BUST A RHYME

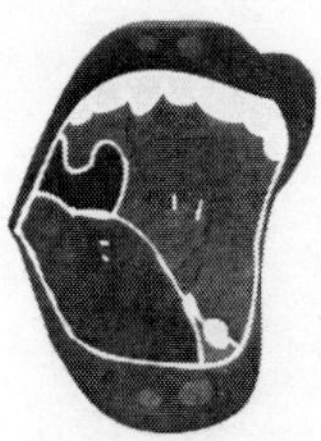

I SHUFFLE THROUGH MY MIND
TO SEE IF I CAN FIND
THE WORDS I LEFT BEHIND
- GREEN DAY

THE WEST MIDLANDS

Edited By Jenni Harrison

First published in Great Britain in 2017 by:

Young Writers
Est. 1991

Coltsfoot Drive
Peterborough
PE2 9BF
Telephone: 01733 890066
Website: www.youngwriters.co.uk

Book Design by Ashley Janson

SB ISBN 978-1-78624-780-3
Printed and bound in the UK by BookPrintingUK
Website: www.bookprintinguk.com
YB0299Y

FOREWORD

Welcome Reader,

For Young Writers' latest competition, *Busta Rhyme,* we challenged secondary school pupils to take inspiration from the world around them, whether from the news, their own lives or even songs, and write a poem on any subject of their choice. They rose to the challenge magnificently, with young writers up and down the country displaying their poetic flair.

We chose poems for publication based on style, expression, imagination and technical skill. The result is this entertaining collection full of diverse and imaginative poetry which covers a variety of topics - from favourite things and seasons to more serious subjects such as bullying and war. Using poetry as their tool, the young writers have taken this opportunity to express their thoughts and feelings through verse. This anthology is also a delightful keepsake to look back on in years to come.

Here at Young Writers our aim is to encourage creativity in the next generation and to inspire a love of the written word, so it's great to get such an amazing response, with some absolutely fantastic poems. I'd like to congratulate all the young poets in this anthology, I hope this inspires them to continue with their creative writing.

Jenni Harrison

CONTENTS

Lyndon School, Solihull

THE POEMS

Live And Let Die

Handsome man meets beautiful girl
Has a beautiful car, drinks Martini stirred
Beautiful girl loves chilled champagne
Impressed by the car, she goes to his room
What happens there is private, between the two
Kisses are shared, words will never tell.

In the morning he leaves, she knows not where
He's hit by truck yet still survives
Another man warns 'stay away from her'
Our man smiles, gets on with his life.
Spinning his Aston like it's a slot car
Reports to his service, a letter for a name.

Never off guard, or where he should be
Dresses so sharp, the finest of gear
Lost his wife to a villain, won't love again
Committed to his country, he hides behind the job
Hopes to die in his work, golf's not for full time
Mr Bond, we expect, will never retire.

J O (13)
Chase House School, Walsall

Identity?

They all try to look the same,
They all try to give themselves a name.
Pick on a boy who is all alone,
Just because his identity is his own.
What has this world come to?
All this wrong that people do.
Just for the image they want to show,
Down the evil path they seem to go.
The next person you go to hurt,
Or try to make them feel like dirt,
Instead of trying to look so cool,
Feel for the guy you make look a fool.
Your identity isn't a need,
Let those you bully be freed.
Your identity should be your own,
A better person will sure to be known.

Name-calling and pushing people around,
Is a victim's nervous breakdown
Fat, ugly, worthless are the words they hear,
You are their biggest fear.
Day by day, you torment them,
It takes so long for hearts to mend.
All they ask is one true friend,
Or their lives to be put to an end.
Every day they wake up with regret,
All they want is to forget.

It isn't the violence, it's just the words you say,
That hurts them much to fade away.
When enough is enough,
They are sick of playing really strong and tough,
They put on a fake smile and pretend it's OK,
Eager to make it all the way.
And of course words still offend.

They pull themselves together again.
Their smile is no longer fake,
Now they have no reason to ache.
Now they are free,
The insults barely sting, don't you see?
Bullying gave you power, that they refused to give,
You can't help but wonder what if?
What if they didn't get so strong?
What if they were crumpled all along?
What if they wrote down secrets they had to spill,
Right before taking an overdose of pills?

You don't know what couldn't been done,
You were doing it all for fun.
You think they're losers, but they are stronger than you,
Have you seen what they've been through?
With your words you gave a black eye,
They are leaving, so say goodbye.

But one more thing, before you go,
Did you enjoy your little show?

Just remember that this is humanity,
Having a good heart is the key to identity.

Mirgan Adel Saeed Ahmed (13)
George Salter Academy, West Bromwich

Unique But Special

Don't judge people every day,
Don't judge people or get carried away
It's hard to explain, it's hard to understand,
But easier to misjudge all the personalities around one land.
Every person is unique,
Every person is special.
Don't try to get in the way or you will hurt their feelings
every day.
Take interests in their beliefs,
Or interest in some other case,
But you might be able to create a smile on someone's face.
If they didn't have different identities
The world wouldn't be so interesting,
Then how would you make friends so rare...
But have lots of care!
Just try to understand
What is going on around you
And you will see how people like you
And would want to be your only friend.
So everyone just take a peek inside your heart,
Maybe it's time to express your inside
To others who will want to realise.
Don't hide, just express!

Hudebia Khalid (15)
George Salter Academy, West Bromwich

Fake Smile

Expectation vs realty
It's like comparing myself to Gigi Hadid
Face, figure, arms, race, it's all better quality
They told me to fix up, all my 'friends' agreed.

Crowds told me I had no meaning in life,
Just because I wasn't tall and slim and model-like.
They made me pick up a knife,
Making me wish I wasn't alive.

I hide myself from the world,
I hide myself from myself.
It makes my posture all miniature and curled,
That's what she said to herself.

Humanity 'advised' me to buy clothes from Prada,
But my dad's showing me the right way of life.
They don't understand that I 'ain't got nada'
All dolled up I'm a cactus and you're a purple-loosestrife.

Beyoncé, Rihanna, Drake,
Oh I know them I'm just not an impersonator.
They're human beings for goodness sake
Killing my confidence, you're my terminator.

Magazines, articles, books.
'Ooh, look at me I'm so fancy'
Judging me on my looks,
To my mum, you make me howl like a banshee

I have so much to say,
Yet I'm too afraid to socialise.
I toss and turn whilst I lay,
I don't have a chance to globalise.

This poem is a voice of a 12-year-old child,
What must she have been going through?
She laughed and fake smiled.
What has this world come to?

Nazia Yeasmin (12)
George Salter Academy, West Bromwich

My School

I love school
And I am cool,
There's loads of great subjects like drama,
Where I can dress up like a farmer.
Also there is English,
Where you get to learn English-based stuff (like poetry)
And there's science where you get to learn the lifecycle of a fish.
I think school is great and I wish,
There's loads of amazing subjects like maths,
Hopefully there's a moment where everybody laughs,
And everybody has fun,
And enjoy in the sun,
History is where you get to learn about the past
And see how it changed so fast,
RE is about religion,
And some religions might believe in reincarnation.
In PE there's all sorts of great sports,
Like football and basketball,
Where anyone can play short or tall.
In technology you make stuff with wood,
In cooking you can make loads of food like pizza,
Which will make you feel good.
ICT is where you use computers.
Always remember to listen to Miss and Sir
Because they're here to help us,

If you don't like a lesson, don't make a fuss,
In music you learn about tone,
But remember in school not to use a phone,
Remember to never give up,
Everybody has good luck.

Azraf Chowdhury (12)
George Salter Academy, West Bromwich

Killer Clowns

Watch! Look out for these ghoulish clowns
Or you will be hunted as prey,
So whatever you do, just be nimble like a cheetah.

They spread, they scare, they choke, but not everyone is a joke,
Murky night, Friday night can this be the last day of your life?
So whatever you do just be nimble like a cheetah.

The outfit that clowns wear are rainbow colours,
So people can see them in the foggy street,
The clowns have cruel kindness so be careful,
So whatever you do just be nimble like a cheetah.

In the circus the clown transforms in a role,
Clowns perform, paint and play in an intimidating way,
As they bang with their food that the rats would be anxious,
So whatever you do just be nimble like a cheetah.

Imagine at dusk you're still busy and there is torrential rain and it is boisterous,
And someone shrieks, you feel frightened and bewildered
You don't support authority.

Abruptly you perceive a benign tap,
With a clap,
Do you think there are two clowns?

You ponder quickly what should I do?
Jump to the sky, rush for life, howl for help or give up and die.
This makes *The Killer Clowns.*

Weronika Zywica (11)
George Salter Academy, West Bromwich

I Stand

Everyone's out for themselves
People blinded by wealth
It's like the world's turned deaf
There's a nation crying for help
Poor kids are getting blown up
Before they're grown up
But still no love
My heart goes numb when the images show up
Brothers and sisters are dying
These politicians are busy deciding
How to divide and conquer
We need to unite and be stronger
And not make the same mistake that we did in 1947
Pakistan and India and a border dividing our ancestors
I stand with Gaza, Palestine, Syria and Ramallah
If you're searching for paradise
It lies below those martyrs,
I'm Muslim, she's Hindu, he's Sikh, she's Christian
Tell me how we are different
Isn't it humanity before religion?
It's clear to understand this
We don't need to speak the same language
There an onslaught massacre
Yet the news shows nothing about it
That's why I refuse to watch the news

My mind gets infected with horror
I stand with Gaza, Palestine, Syria and Ramallah
If you're searching for Paradise
It lies below those martyrs.

Ifzal Jabar (12)
George Salter Academy, West Bromwich

Equality

There's over 1.6 billion people in this world with greater insecurities
Yet you choose to judge me because of my nationality?
Just because I'm a different race
Just because I have a different face
You shouldn't be judging me in the first place so tell me,
What's a human being to do
With the fact that you
Treat me like I'm some sort of rat
But in reality it's you who's messing with my mentality
So what have I got to do to get some equality?
Every day many people die inside
Just because of hatred
They have to hide
Ripping apart lives will get you nowhere
Only if you tried to care
Words, yells, screams and taunts
As you know, they do haunt
Self-esteem is their target
And I will let them at it
They echo in mind
You start to think it's not a lie
Day after day it goes on, with no stop
All muddled in one huge knot
The stones and knives you throw at me

Will no longer harm me
Because now I will show you
The true meaning of
Equality.

Roopjot Malhi (13)
George Salter Academy, West Bromwich

How Do You Think It Feels?

How do you think it feels,
When people call you names?
How do you think it feels,
Those people getting fame?
When those people hurt you inside they leave a scar forever,
They want your forgiveness, but you can't say never.

How do you think it feels,
When people call you fat?
How do you think it feels,
When you try to hide?
All of my life I can't put on a hat,
Even when I'm walking past you
You don't even mind.

How do you think it feels,
When you're standing all alone?
How do you think it feels,
When you have no one to phone?
You can act like you don't care,
You can try to hold strong,
But the feelings inside you are too hard to ignore.

How do you think it feels,
When you try to act cool?
How do you think it feels

When you feel like a fool?
No one to turn to, well look at me now,
You bullied me then, shame on you!

Katie Simms (11)
George Salter Academy, West Bromwich

Perfection

Take this deal,
Sign it with red
Use one of these drops,
Which I have bled

I'm tired of everything,
Now do you see
What all this nonsense
Is doing to me?

My sanity is slipping,
Slowly losing its hold
Like in a game of poker,
I'm sure it will fold

I'm on the verge,
Of losing everything I had
All because I messed up,
And did something bad.

I'm sorry I'm not,
The perfect child,
But could you please understand,
That I will never be for a while?

Perfection is a goal,
Something you desire
But like a normal person,
We all stand too close to the fire

Dreaming of something,
That we can never gain
Throughout this journey,
There's nothing but pain

The truth comes out,
Nobody's perfect
So in the end of it all,
Is the pain really worth it?

Anisah Tasnim (12)
George Salter Academy, West Bromwich

Crime

That's it, I'm done with this, there's no point of it,
That's why we have school not being a fool and having duels,
Getting drunk and eating junk will mess us up,
You think losing cash won't do that bad then we will see about that.

All these clowns running around making the public cry out loud,
All these horrible people are gonna get found,
Stealing money they think they're funny even when it's really sunny,
That's it, I have had enough.

Going to jail is worse than standing in hail,
When they try stealing it's mostly a big, fat fail,
Then they're going around getting luxury and money using blackmail
Drugs, drugs, drugs, no point, just go to the pet shop and go buy a pug.

Losing family, losing friends,
The ones who helped and dealt,
This is how it all ends,
It's a horrible world out there,
That's it, I have had enough.

Amanveer Singh Sangha (13)
George Salter Academy, West Bromwich

Follow Your Heart

On the first of June,
When I flew to the moon
About to take a picture,
But then I pressed zoom.

Crash-landed on Mars,
All I could see was bright, blue stars
Turned around and saw my spaceship dead
How was this tragic news meant to spread?

My journey was almost done,
All I had to do was hit the sun.
I would have saved each and everyone.

I flew to Jupiter, Saturn, Neptune and now Mars,
Which was the only one that broke my heart.
I didn't want to be an astronaut at the start,
I wanted to follow my dreams and become a pop star.

But my mom told me to follow my heart,
Now I got myself in this mess,
I can't even get myself dressed.

Because I'm living in a world with no gravity,
And I've got nobody to play with me.

Talib Copeland (12)
George Salter Academy, West Bromwich

Why You Love This World

Why do we hurt each other?
Why don't we love one another?
War, glory, violence,
That's what haters think makes
The world spin.

You don't have to hate
You don't have to kill
You just need to love.

Love the gays, bisexuals and
Love the blacks and whites.
Love the family that supports you
Love everything to set things right.

This Earth we stand on can
Be our Saviour, our God,
Yet the ones filled with hate
Want to destroy our people, individuality
And the air we love.

World, planets, humans,
Humanity is one and shouldn't be
Divided into groups
But we should love each other as one.

Through these attacks you believe that love is still there
And you see how everyone across the world is supporting each other,
And that's why you love this world.

Nicole Withers (14)
George Salter Academy, West Bromwich

Lost Love!

When a person you love
Walks out of the door
Like a fish swimming out to sea
It's heartbreaking that the person
You love can suddenly not love me.

When they worry about a little thing
It's amazing that they don't love you
It's not because you have done something wrong
So don't change yourself
Just be true.

When the person you love is spending time with another
It's not you who he wants anymore
So pick yourself up and brush yourself down
Don't try to reopen the door.

So don't be upset, just leave him alone
He is an idiot can't you see?
Don't change for a man, just be yourself
One day you'll find someone lovely.

The world is beautiful just like you
He must be stupid to let you go
Let him be stupid, let him walk out
He'll miss you when he is low.

Jenna Payton (12)
George Salter Academy, West Bromwich

Black And White

Two different contrasting colours; both equal!
The colours balance each other out:
They help each other in order to preserve Earth.
Although opposites, very similar,
I speak both tongues of black and white.
You might think opposites attract,
Think again!
The two different colours can lead to love, passion, hate or discrimination.
Our opinions and views are as different as black and white, yes it's true but,
We're the same beneath: no one should be valued less:
Unfortunately in this world discrimination still happens.
I am not black, it's you who's white.
You were just taught to call me that.
From birth we are given the labels black or white,
To me, that's the judgemental mind of Mother Earth.
Who we truly are is not skin deep.
However the truth still remains,
I am black and you are white.

Hilda Alade (12)
George Salter Academy, West Bromwich

Does It Relate To You?

They don't get it...
He doesn't get it,
She doesn't get it,
No one gets it...

You won't get it
Till you have it

We want to educate children
Tell them how common it is
But how is that even possible
If we're afraid to talk about it?

We need to work on first
Pushing bullies away
To not know what you're feeling
It's completely okay.

We feel like we can't talk
But why can we not talk?
It's not like we killed someone!
We are still normal

Have you ever noticed
That I haven't talked about it?
I've said we need to let it out,
But I haven't actually said it

The thing that everyone
Thinks is complete taboo
Is mental health
Does it relate to you?

Morgan Louisa Grice (14)
George Salter Academy, West Bromwich

Be Who You Are

Everyone telling you how to be
Magazines showing pictures of people who are pretty
Changing your body
But it is not for you; it is not for you
Be who you are!

Everyone telling you how to be
Judging you by your cover
So you try to act cool
But you are just acting like a fool
Be who you are!

Everyone telling you how to be
They say you're ugly
They say your body isn't right
But they don't know how you are feeling inside
Be who you are!

Everyone telling you how to be
They saying you're not so pretty
You try to be positive
Ends up being negative
Be who you are!

Everyone telling you how to be
Don't listen to them
Listen to me
Don't let them tell you how to be
Be who you are!

Anum Khan (12)
George Salter Academy, West Bromwich

Education Is The Key To Life!

Education
The key to a bright and rewarding future
A glue that joins our dreams like a suture
Education
The process of teaching and learning
Which will help us in our future earning
Education
The key to unlock the golden door of freedom
And the stage of our rise to stardom
Education
A fundamental foundation
For any country, state or nation
Education
A thick line between right and wrong
A ladder that takes us to the height where we belong
Education
A path to divine success
A smooth drive to our greatness
Education
Not all about bookish knowledge
But it is also about a practical knowledge
Education
Mother of all profession

That helps us to acquire all our possession
Education
Education is our right
For in it, our future is bright.

Shriya Dora (14)
George Salter Academy, West Bromwich

Her Brother

Walking through the door,
She calls for her brother,
She doesn't get an answer,
So she calls for her mother.

She turns around,
With a tear in her eye,
She receives a message,
And starts to cry.

The message was,
'Your brother has died,
There was nothing we could do,
Except for lie.'

A few months back,
When you were at school,
He had a heart transplant,
But then we got the news.

His disease had spread,
Quicker than others,
There was nothing we could do,
For your poor, poor brother.

He cherished you,
Just like I do,
And told me,
To 'Take care of you.'

And now she's older,
As old as he was,
She looks back at photos,
And thinks how awesome he was.

Zeba Qazafi (12)
George Salter Academy, West Bromwich

War

It's a big thing war,
People's families are getting torn,
Why was it all caused?
I think they need to stop and pause.

Stop and think about life,
Instead of using a knife.
Killing is not an answer,
It hurts like dying of cancer.

Boom! There goes more men
Why is there so much bloodshed?
Tears fall down men's faces
Why is it such a bad case?

But they will always be our heroes,
And none of them are worth zero.
They fought for me and for you,
What else could they possibly do?
When they sleep they think about tomorrow

And when you look in their eyes
They are filled with horror
No-Man's-Land is what they call it, the battleground.
They were brave heroes,
And none of them are worth zero.

Kazia Emily Niemczyk (12)
George Salter Academy, West Bromwich

Never Lose Your Identity

You try'na find my identity,
Well no,
You can't stoop that low.
My mom says don't change yourself.
She says it's good to be you,
Not anyone else.

You try'na meet, try'na text, try'na phone me.
What's wrong now, you feeling lonely,
Leaving me behind just like I'm a phoney.
You try and stab me every single day.
It's like you want some money,
You want me to pay.

At the end of the day,
It would always end my way.
You say, 'Kay' in the middle of May.
You hurt me, punch me, and give me some scars,
I'm like no, but I'll give you some tarts.

In the end we'll make sure we're friends.
We'll say forget this manner,
We'll make sure it mends.

Vina Younis (12)
George Salter Academy, West Bromwich

My Luxury Life

Once I was poor,
You know what, begged for a PS4,
You know what they say,
Stop trying because you can't afford it.

I started working one day,
The amount was a good pay,
That was when I thought that was good,
That was when I thought that I should.

Everything was good but one day when I said, 'Oh my gosh.'
I thought what a loss,
Got good money,
Bought a 6.3 litre Ferrari Enzo.

I thought one day I could be a millionaire,
Maybe even a billionaire,
Bought a mansion,
I thought, *what else do I need?*

Gave money to Water Aid,
Won't believe how much I paid,
Gave a mil to them,
Imagine what that could do to them.

This was the story to my luxury life.

Ismail Mohammed Ajmal (12)
George Salter Academy, West Bromwich

Peace

Isn't 'cause I follow Islam,
I guess that makes me a terrorist, a Taliban.
Every day people are getting killed,
Kill 'em with silence, react blindness,
No shots need to be fired.

This now concludes the battle against good and evil,
Now people are leaving their country and coming to Europe;
They've got no mother or father, no brother or sister,
No shelter or cover.
Sitting in the dark on unknown streets.

What's the point if you're trying to act bad
Like you run the scene
When in fact you forget about your Deen.
Islam is the religion of inner peace,
We pray 5 times a day.
We give to charity to release
We travel to pilgrimage, we fast in Ramadan,
Being a Muslim makes me a happy man.

Abdul Ahmed (11)
George Salter Academy, West Bromwich

Why Me?

Why is it me that you always bully?
Why are you the person who tries to scare me?
Why does it happen when nobody is near?
The taunts and words that no one can hear!

I can't keep letting you ruin my life,
The things you say cut as deep as a knife,
I know I have to keep being strong,
This bullying has gone on for far too long!

I've found the courage to pick up the phone,
I know I can't stop this on my own,
It's time for me to make a stand,
It's time to ask for a helping hand
To tell a teacher, parent or Childline,
To get back the life that is rightfully mine.

Your fists don't hurt me,
Your words won't scar,
You don't scare me,
I will go far!

Bethany Knight (12)
George Salter Academy, West Bromwich

Education

Sitting and doing your work is very difficult,
But others around the world, die for an education,
Some women around the world, want an education,
But they are forced to be slaves in different areas,
Many days you might hate school,
But others around you might say it's cool,
Always think of those around the world,
Who have to work with big, heavy tools.
Reading and writing will take you a long way,
Into the future until the end of the day.
When you are reading all you can see are words,
But in your brain you see a new world!
An education can lead to a good job.
And in that job, you can make a friend named Bob!
Always remember, in life you need one thing... *education!*

Nabiha Sana Imran (12)
George Salter Academy, West Bromwich

Just Wait

It's not right,
To ever fight,
With someone who,
You never knew,
Just because
Someone does
Something you don't like,
Or if they steal your bike.

It makes you as bad as them
Just wait,
Don't walk through that gate,
They'll get bored,
They won't think they're a lord
Just if you say,
That brave word,
They'll stop calling you a nerd,

Stop.

It does a lot,
You'll borrow books you've got,
The world will be happy,
You'll both be clappy,
With your new friend,
You will have emails to send.

By being nice,
There is no price,
And by being kind,
The world will bind.

Armandas Spokas (11)
George Salter Academy, West Bromwich

No Love In War

Doesn't matter the type of war,
Heartache and misery we can't ignore,
They put their lives on the line,
Blood and dirt there is no shine,
With every single fearful breath,
Seconds and seconds closer to their deaths,
Never heard so many cries,
All you see is sorrow in everyone's eyes,
This has affected so many lives,
Children, parents, husbands and wives,
Dead bodies lay in pools of blood,
Soldiers marching all covered in mud,
Everywhere you look dead bodies lay,
Sunshine is gone, you can only see grey
Looking around thinking is this real?
Desperate for silence and a good meal,
Looking up as the sky turns greyer,
Think of them and say a prayer.

Umar Miah (12)
George Salter Academy, West Bromwich

My Request To You

Oh Lord, please help me
To make those kids see,
Who I really am,
Since this all began.
Lord, what can I do?
I'm giving it all to You.
This is my request,
Nothing more, nothing less.
Don't wanna go to school,
But my dad says, 'Don't be a fool!'
Just make me stronger,
For a little bit longer.
'Til I know for sure,
That You've planned for more.
Please don't refuse
Don't let them accuse
The person You made.
Don't let me fade
Into ashes of nothing.
You gotta do something,
Cos what did I do wrong?
It's like a big gong -
Ringing in my ears
Lord, take away my fears.

Jebisha Daniel
George Salter Academy, West Bromwich

Dad!

Dad, I miss you with all my heart,
I hate that we are torn apart,
Always remembered and never forgotten,
You might be dead but to me you're not rotten,
First words were always spoken,
And you were never there when I awoke,
First steps were taken,
But my heart was always breaking

Our bond will never be the same again,
But I'll always be happy when I hear your name,
Why did you have to go so soon,
Why couldn't you wait till full moon?

When Mum said that you were gone,
I told her that she was wrong.
Until we meet again,
Rest in peace,
And you will always be in my sweet, sweet dreams.

Tseyon Gebreselassie (12)
George Salter Academy, West Bromwich

Crime

You better watch out through the day
They won't care what you say
You better watch out through the night
You don't know who's waiting to give you a fright.
You don't know whether you will be stabbed by a knife,
Or be clinging on for dear life.
Turn on the TV
What do you see
I know what I see
And it scares me deeply
Because you don't know how long your life will last
You could be killed ever so fast.
Everyone's going to die
And they will regret living a lie
What is left in this world? Crime
And we all have to pay the time.
If you're evil you won't truly survive
Your inner demon will eat you alive!

Ethan Johnson (12)
George Salter Academy, West Bromwich

What Has Happened?

Why doesn't anyone care?
Why doesn't anyone care about the world?
Why doesn't anyone care about anything?
What has this world come to?

Everyone needs to open their eyes and see reality,
They need to see what's going on around them.
Everyone needs to help out as a team!

There are lots of things that are happening around the world
Deforestation, pollution, capturing animals for humans to see,
Earthquakes, poverty and many more.

We all need to open our eyes
We all need to see what is happening
We all need to help out
We all need to work as a team!

Maisha Haque (12)
George Salter Academy, West Bromwich

You Are Your Own Host!

When love turns into hate,
It is only your fate.
You need to show them yourself,
That you're not their little elf.

It's time for you to get new friends,
To realise it's not your end.
To be perfect is their aim,
They think life is just a game.

Soon they will face the wrath of reality,
And find out we're just following morality.
Even if you think there is a reason
It is never the season.

Even if it hurts inside,
Put it behind you, or to the side.
Love the people that treasure you the most,
Don't forget you are your own host.

Jessica Busby (12)
George Salter Academy, West Bromwich

Human Rights!

Is it because of my skin?
Is it because of who I am?
Is it because of where I'm from?
Everyone gets treated differently.
Some people are thinner,
Some people are thicker
Some people of different colours
We all might be different
But we are all humans.
Some get treated different
Because of who we are
Just because of who we are
Doesn't mean we are all bizarre.
Some people get judged on who they are
When they get judged they become insecure.
Is it because of my skin?
Is it because of who I am?
Is it because of where I am from?
We are who we are!

Lemia Murray (12)
George Salter Academy, West Bromwich

#BringBackOldFeminism

Try as you might,
You can never reason with them.
We call them 'Feminazis'
We do this for a reason.

They say stupid things,
And wish death upon people.
Thinking they're above consequences
Believing no one but their mothers.

Saying that men are the scum of the Earth
Attempting to shift the blame onto others,
'#KIllallmen is the key
To lift all of our bothers!'

'But, men are all the same,
Judging people based on their sex'
Well times have changed,
And so should our mindsets.

Jack Beasley (13)
George Salter Academy, West Bromwich

Anxiety

I feel a red flush wash over my face
Like a tsunami
I succumb to the frightening thoughts
In my mind.
Obsessed with the way I look,
The way I dress,
Always desperate to impress
My chest goes tight and
My stomach's in knots
My head starts spinning and my body goes hot.
Panic girl. Stress head.
Sometimes I can't even get myself out of bed.
Isolated at school,
I feel like I'm drowning in the deep end of a pool.
Enemies, friends, they merge into one
Like a sea full of sharks and they all smell blood.

Lexy Brazier (13)
George Salter Academy, West Bromwich

Women

Women being like slaves
Not allowed to work
Shedding skin as their arms
Scrubbing down the floor.

Didn't get a GCSE
Got married at 14
Skills to learn all
All on their own.

Mothers at 16
Don't know how to be a mother
But she has to learn
Or it is the end of the line.

Wanting the best for child
But nothing she can do.
There in-laws shout, the baby wakes,
The routine goes on.

The baby is ill,
Sleepless nights
What else can she do
Except hate life.

Samayah Manzoor (12)
George Salter Academy, West Bromwich

Welcome To Society

(Inspired by 'Welcome to Society' by Erin Hanson)

Welcome to Society
This is now your place to stay
There are no rules here
But you have to do what we say
And please feel free to be yourself
As long as in our eyes it looks alright
We are here if you need us
But we won't always listen
We'll only be there when it's your time to glisten
We'll call you worthless
We'll make you frown
Then cry with all the others
As you're placed underground
Welcome to Society
We promise we won't deceive
One more rule now you're here
There is no way you can leave.

Nayima Sadiq (12)
George Salter Academy, West Bromwich

It's A Life

You think it's a game,
But you don't see the pain,
All their troubles in their life,
But what happens when they pull out a knife,

Words and hate will go away,
But scars and cuts are there to stay,
You see the smiles, not the tears,
From many, many years,

You think it's not your time,
But this isn't just a silly rhyme,
It's a life that matters,
Even if it shatters,

You're a charm,
So don't self-harm,
Live your life the way you want to live it,
Don't kill it.

Charlotte Davies (12)
George Salter Academy, West Bromwich

Isn't It Funny

How some special people don't realise they're special at all?
Because of you, I laugh a little harder,
Cry a little less, and smile a lot more.
My best friend is worth more than gold
Giving all the love a heart can hold.
Together we party, together we cry
Kept every single secret until we die.
You're my best friend, you were from the start
Together we stand strong, we shall never part.
Many people will walk in and out of my life
But only a true friend will leave footprints in my heart.

Mya Gohir (12)
George Salter Academy, West Bromwich

Environment

The environment should be clean, tidy and litter-free,
Environment is a place for everyone to see,
The environment should be looked after,
The community should be full of laughter.

The environment should be clean,
The environment should be tidy,
The environment should look nice,
The environment is our world we live in.

The environment should be clean,
The environment should be tidy,
So don't treat it like a big party,
The message is look after your environment
And treat it with care and love.

Launa Tyson (13)
George Salter Academy, West Bromwich

Just Because I'm Different

I'm only 13,
My whole life's ahead of me,
I hate school because the people there discredit me.

My best friend tries to show me that's not how it seems,
But every day I just get lowered with my self-esteem.

Words are like knives and often leave scars,
I just wish the bullies were put behind bars.

I don't know why these words cause so much pain,
But I know it will come back like the blood in my veins.

I rise above it flying high,
And soon enough I won't feel shy.

Fallon Wilcox (12)
George Salter Academy, West Bromwich

Man's Best Friend And You

I'm not just a present
I'm not just a toy
I may not be so pleasant
I am just for you

The name you give me
Is the name that stays
If that name changes
Then don't just say

Give me a crumb
Give me a biscuit
Give me some love
'Cause I will always need it

So I'm not just some dog
I'm yours to love
So when you see me
Love me

I'm not just a present
I'm your lifelong pal
I'm your dog
And you're my pal.

Joshua Aldred (14)
George Salter Academy, West Bromwich

Bullying

That boy you punched in the hall today.
Slits his wrist because he faces depression.
The boy you called dumb.
He has to work every night to support his family.
That girl you pushed down the other day.
Is already being abused at home.
That girl you called fat.
She's starving herself.
That old man you made fun of because of his scars.
He fought for our country.
That boy you made fun of for crying.
His mother is dying.
You think you know them.
Guess what, you don't!

Adam Isaac Dawkins (11)
George Salter Academy, West Bromwich

Anxiety

Thoughts race through my head

Like a constant door knocking loudly
I can't ask for another drink at restaurants
It's like I'm a needle
Lost in a haystack

Anxiety...
It can be more than emotions
It can be physical and even painful
And it can lead to you wanting
Well, things you shouldn't.

People think that they understand,
But they can't possibly understand.
People think they know how it feels.

But it just lasts forever.

Sinead Debbie Hayes (12)
George Salter Academy, West Bromwich

War Is Useless

You see them fighting for land,
Covered in sand,
Dead bodies flying,
While innocent people are crying,

The soldiers are terrified,
Since they have to decide,
Should they kill millions
And endanger even more civilians,

Just for a piece of dry land,
A useless piece of land,
Which causes millions of civilians to die,
And their families to cry,

War is useless,
It does no good,
It takes innocent people's lives,
Because people misunderstood.

Arif Rahman (12)
George Salter Academy, West Bromwich

The Clowns!

Be scared, be prepared,
They are coming just for you,
Who? The clowns?
The big, scary clowns.

They carry a knife, gun, axe,
It doesn't matter,
Because they come day and night,
They don't stop until you die,

They thirst for blood,
They hide in forests,
If you try to find them
They will find you first,

They are just around the corner,
Waiting to pop out,
To drag you into the forest
Where you will never see the light again.

Matiass Gertners (12)
George Salter Academy, West Bromwich

Dream

As I sat on a jade laden hill
An essence of beauty incarnate
Walked by.

As I stood up my heart throbbed
I gazed into her sapphire eyes
I saw a glimmer of hope
Amidst the dark thoughts
That stalked me.

As I turned and gazed at darkness
I floated towards a starlit Heaven.
Then I gazed back
My eyes turned to hearts, my body to stone.

But as I came too I realised
It was a dream and nothing more
But a figment of my imagination.

Deshawn Fortune-Creary (13)
George Salter Academy, West Bromwich

No One Is Perfect

Why are we like this?
Why do we stare?
Why does this image inside our head scare?

Are we too fat?
Or are we too thin?
All these images on the Internet,
Are they going to win?

Social media has ruined our life,
With all these fake images for us to like.
Perfect hair, perfect smile,
It only lasts for a little while.

So, stop this bullying,
What have they done?
No one is perfect,
So please, be gone.

Molly Dodd (12)
George Salter Academy, West Bromwich

Equal

I am you in another body!
Yes it's true,
Look how much the same we are,
No mater what,
The colour,
The creed,
The race,
The status.

Look,
I am born and die,
Suffer and enjoy,
Love and hate,
Just like you.

I am a father,
A brother, a son,
A mother, a sister,
A daughter,
Just like you.

Happiness I seek,
Family to raise,
Peace to find I look for
Just like you.

Safwan Imad (12)
George Salter Academy, West Bromwich

Leave Me Alone!

Kicking, punching, taunting me
When will I be safe and free?
Tears fall so I curl up tightly like a ball.
When I'm angry I punch a wall.
When will these people leave me alone
I wish I had someone I could call my own.
Wishing crying, praying I am tired of saying.
Calling names it's driving me insane.
Filling me up with lots of shame.
Wish I'd said something sooner
Now it's too late
Why is this world so full of hate?

Alisha Devi Sanyar (14)
George Salter Academy, West Bromwich

Advantages

They twist, they turn,
They moan, they groan,
But still they have to learn.

They have it after everything they eat.
Advantages.
Things they take for granted
Lies.
Every girl.
Advantages.

They help out,
They don't mess about.
But still, they earn to learn,
They get it sometimes as a treat.
Advantages
Things they want but don't get.
Tales.
Every male
Things they don't get.

Aleesha Francis (12)
George Salter Academy, West Bromwich

Untitled

They slapped me in the face,
Trying to put me in my place.
They think I'm a disgrace,
Someone they want to replace.
Every day I feel pain,
Sadness flowing through my veins.

Each time I wake up tears roll down my face,
I tremble in the corner of my bed.
Vicious voices booming from downstairs,
Giving me orders,
Calling me names.
Making me feel like nothing
Again! Repeat!

Luke Hall (12)
George Salter Academy, West Bromwich

Fairies

Oh my god fairies are real
Now I know, I keep my eyes peeled
Every night they fly by me
I really wonder, what could they be?

Are they pretty? Are they ugly?
Are they cute? Are they snuggly?
Are they angry? Are they calm?
Could I keep them in my palm?

Do you think I'll ever know?
Will they ever let themselves go?

Rasha Salah Nasir (11)
George Salter Academy, West Bromwich

War Solves Nothing

Why do people fight?
They're just risking their life,
Because war solves nothing...
People are dying
And their loved ones crying,
Because war solves nothing...
Soldiers falling to the ground
Hopeless and making no sound,
Because war solves nothing...
Respect the people who are dying
Because they keep our flag flying.

Manraj Singh (12)
George Salter Academy, West Bromwich

US Police Politics

He wakes up feeling sound and healthy
Sounds of sirens filling his brain
He's used to this, so he ignores
He kneels down and starts to pray
Until he's interrupted by the sound of a police officer shouting
'Come out, it's all going to be okay!'
He stands up and hears a sweeter voice asking him, 'What's the matter?'
But this gentle voice is coming from the mouth of his brown-skinned daughter.
He smiles and says, 'Nothing wrong sweetie'
She smiles back but inside she's feeling sadder
He heads downstairs, every step sounding harder
As he opens the door
He sees nothing else than a group of policemen holding him at gunpoint
They shout, 'Lie down with your head facing downwards'
As he does this, he hears the door shut
'My kids are here, please stop'
As he cries, the police officer searches him up
In this moment as a black man he knows he has no hope
So he lets them do their 'job'.
As he is searched nothing is found
What a surprise
The police officer says he's free to go
Apologises for being wrong

But as he steps back he's shot,
His wife shouts, 'Jesus Christ!'

The only thing that could have saved this man, sadly,
Was if he was white.

Elisha Prince Ogwo Eme (14)
Grace Academy, Coventry

Desires And False Personas

I stand here in front of you,
A fourteen-year-old boy belittled by my own presence,
With a burning desire to be accepted.
And as I stand here I wonder,
Are you the real you?

For one, I know for sure that I am the real me,
At least the side you know.
But the thing is your thoughts are not mine,
And the way you see me I will eventually control,
I with little to no hope to die.

When I leave, I want people to remember me.
They'll say I had a 'smiley frown',
A walking oxymoron.
Although they'll probably leave out the oxy!

Oh well,

I wish my words made a change,
If I could, I'd lyrically repent every audience to believe what was right.
No hate toward gay, white, straight, black, big, fat, thin, or 'foreign',
It wouldn't matter.

But I'll keep on rhyming like I've committed a crime!
A sentence spent confined inside these walls,
These gates that probably used to shine,

But now, they are rusted and old.

My dad would tell me to be bold,
Funny, because he is bald! and hasn't had hair for most of my life.

I've gone off rhyming now,

We're done.

Jobe Alldrick (14)
Grace Academy, Coventry

Dying World

Our vast environment is an extraordinary spectacle,
But to save it, that's going to take a miracle,
We humans are destroying and attacking our land,
It's humans versus humans but the environmental protectors are unmanned,
Industrialisation, pollution, deforestation, global warming, our biggest threats,
The thought of those increasing even more gives me a cold sweat,
Climate change is leading us on our path to mayhem and chaos,
Soon our population is going to decrease and descend, and won't that be a loss?
More floods, tsunamis, natural disasters arising all over the earth,
Our people are going to die making us think, is it even worth having birth?
With ignorance and a blind eye, world leaders let it stand,
Being in denial, thinking things are fine, in some sort of dreamland,
Bangs and blows our world is being constantly hit,
Screams and blood, a consequence to what we have let people commit,
Mother Nature is suffering, how much more to endure?
The pain that's been inflicted, no sign of a cure,
Whilst the world is being attacked, taking its final deathly blows,
Are we doing enough to stop this destruction?... The answer is no.

Ethan Richard Connolly (17)
Grace Academy, Coventry

What Do You See?

You see that boy walking to his next class.
Others laugh as he walks past,
Just because he wears pink
Because according to everyone he's obviously queer.
Religion walks past and cowers in fear,
Newsflash, he's straight.
But what difference should that make?

Over there, see that guy?
Just sitting there drinking his coffee.
Well honestly tell me what to do you see?
Just because he's got darker skin.
That means he's honestly going to take your life.
With that gorgeous sharp, silver blade of a butcher's knife,
And turn it crimson red.
Red from the blood of racism and hate.

Watch that girl walk to her house,
Beaming smile, invisible tears,
As she tries to escape Media's grasp.
It shouts out thinner, taller and prettier.
Brainwashed by the stars.
The only things that remain of her true self are the scars.
So just give yourself a round of applause.
As you may not see it yet but you're the real cause.

Rachel Leach (14)
Grace Academy, Coventry

Is He Still Standing There?

Monday I saw him standing there,
To see his face... I couldn't bear.
Words couldn't describe my fear,
I could sense that he was near.

Tuesday he was standing there,
I saw him in my nightmare.
How long would he wait
Before I met my fate?

Wednesday I knew he was standing there,
I won't talk to him, I swear!
His yellow eyes like a snake,
As he watched me at my wake.

Thursday he was standing there,
I guess I'll never know.
As I'm six feet underground,
My hair as white as snow.

Friday I wonder if he's standing there,
No one knows and no one cares.
Now he's gotten away with his crime.
While I'm deteriorating and covered in grime.

Saturday I heard him standing there,
This time my heart can't beat.
The red can't flush into my cheeks,
This time he can't hear me weep.

Sunday is he still standing there?
Years and years have passed,
I haven't seen his golden eyes.
My heart is smashed at last,
At least I'm away from all his lies.
So now I hear his cries...

Lucyleigh Duncan (12) & Alexis
Grace Academy, Coventry

Why?

Why do people think it is okay,
to talk about others every day?
Why is there a problem for them being alive?
Gay, lesbian, trans we all should survive.

Why don't you realise how many lives you're taking,
If someone says they're depressed you always assume they're faking!
Why do you think you are the queen.
On the inside you are uglier than you seem.

Why do we fight like dog and cat?
Can't we just get over all of that?
Why do you have to abuse your wife?
For you she would give up her life.

Why should we all be the same?
Don't you think it would be so lame?
Why do you hate the colour of skin?
Does it really matter if they're thick or thin?

Why do you have to stop and stare?
Because that girl's got no hair,
Why do you think it was her choice?
Do you know cancer has taken her voice?

Why can't you just understand?
Can't we just walk hand in hand?
Why can't we fight together?
Against this terror that might last forever...

Jessica Eve Doyle (12) & Megan Clarke (13)
Grace Academy, Coventry

Sickness In Society

What is discrimination?
Discrimination is judging,
Discrimination is horrible,
Discrimination can turn into bullying.

Bullying is everywhere in school, on social media
And just in society. People make others feel down about themselves.
By doing disgraceful discrimination and brutal bullying.

What is the world becoming?
It's disgusting, it's scary.
Sexism, racism and judgement, you just can't do right
In this world today.

I feel irritated,
I feel puzzled,
I feel dismayed,
It's just sad how people can do this to others, it's not right, it's just not right.
Why would people want to put others down?
It's disgraceful, disrespectful.

People get judged by age, sex, religion and race
Everybody is their own person. Everybody is equal
Everybody has the same rights. It just puzzles me,
How people can treat people like that?
It's wrong!

Courtney McClean (14)
Grace Academy, Coventry

Care Home

He had got rejected
From the house he was ejected
He was in care
But didn't want to be there
He had a mother but not a father
When it came to raising him they didn't bother
He had said when it's gone
And it's done, you are my moonlight
And I am your son
He kept wishing his mum held his hand
For as long as she can
He wished his mum's love never got lost
And that she didn't have to pay the cost
He wished his mum had watched him play
He wished she would care for him each day
For his mum he had strong feelings
But his heart just kept peeling
He tries to set his mind free
But thinking about his mum is killing him
He does not know how to act
But inside his heart was still unpacked
One day he was very happy
As his mum had sent a letter
That she's sorry and everything will get better.

Ayomide Bamgbose (12)
Grace Academy, Coventry

The Martial Arts Team

Here is my passion,
Where most of my friends are
They're all different,
Some are younger,
Some are older,
Some are even Masters.
It doesn't mean they're faster
Or wiser.
As more friends come
More go
We still remember them
That shows our loyalty
But we're not always loyal
Sometimes we are competitive
The championships
Happen all around the world
In Germany,
England
France
And even Wales.
These show our determination
It's not about winning
It's about trying your best.
Then you can achieve anything.
You can achieve safety
Which is the most important thing in Martial Arts.

This shows your independence
And perseverance.
In the end
This all shows
Teamwork and friendship
As we work together.
With all my friends in a massive team
Of hundreds and hundreds.

Keira Patrick (11)
Grace Academy, Coventry

Judgement

School is a place, a place this poem begins,
A place to learn around all different skins,
Where a boy doesn't feel he truly belongs in the student's team,
But in his own world alone, a world in-between,
Judgement.

This boy was from Africa you see,
And felt he was different from you and me,
Every day the other boys would chant their insults and their calls,
As the cruel laughter danced around, bounced off the walls,
Judgement.

He would leave school crying pearly, white tears
Trying, trying to reject his fears and the pain in his eyes
As his heart slowly dies,
Judgement.

The bullies think that white people are better,
But if truth be told, we are all equal,
Whether you're fat, small, slim or tall,
Never judge a book by its cover.

Rachel Bagley (11)
Grace Academy, Coventry

Image

Just because she's different from you,
Playing football and doing what the boys do,
Living in a house filled with boys,
Just because she's different,
It doesn't make it wrong.

Just because she has talent,
And wears shorts and isn't unbalanced,
Having a background with such deep meaning,
Just because she has talent,
It doesn't make it wrong.

Just because she's smart,
And rides a horse and cart,
Living a life,
With such a fight,
Just because she's smart
It doesn't make it wrong.

Just because she goes to work,
And sees the massive jerk,
Finding it hard to cope,
Helping her friend who has no hope
Just because she goes to work,
Does it make it wrong?

Clarice Kidd (14)
Grace Academy, Coventry

Me, Myself And I

I wander around the school,
Feeling anything but cool,
As I wonder to myself,
Am I far beyond help?
Because it's just me, myself and I.

As I get home alone,
Feeling out of the zone,
Wondering if I,
Have the urge to cry,
Because it's just me, myself and I.

As I'm at school,
I just don't feel cool,
Do I have special needs?
Do I know how to say please?
Because it's just me, myself and I.

I feel so alone,
Completely out of the zone,
The goods, the bads,
Just make me feel so sad
Because it's just me, myself and I.

As the drama unfolds,
Even though I'm not that old,
Lots of things happen to me,
And it makes me feel 19,
But it's just me, myself and I.

Emily Davies (12)
Grace Academy, Coventry

How Can We Get Through The Day

How can we get through the day?
Having the courage to wake up every morning, face the same things
Over and over again,
Is a strong thing to do.

You'll face your darkness and paradise
You'll realise getting out of bed was worth getting through
You will have the days where you're feeling broken
Yet again none of these feelings can be spoken
You'll have the days where you pretend you're strong
To hide the fact everything is going wrong.

Things get better, you can be happy again
Keep your head up and smile through the pain
Hmm, how can we get through the day?
Open your eyes, think positive, you'll have nothing negative to say.

Line Mansour (14)
Grace Academy, Coventry

Thinking Of War

War. What is war?
War is no cure, children are hurt,
And they always have the same pain.
In one second the world has changed,
And made all life as dark as a cave.
I've always wondered, what is war?
What is the difference between white, black.
Religious or not, we are all the same
Propaganda, media are all looking for the cash
And the coins to make the same pain.

Everyone has a pattern of life that's like a chain,
Once it ends you can't make a different change
Everyone is looking for a good reason to stop this aim,
If you're black, white, religious or not,
We all have the right to make a stop.
I still wonder: what is war?

Farah Mansour (13)
Grace Academy, Coventry

Trick Or Treat?

Trick or treat?
Ghouls, monsters, werewolves,
Vampires, zombies, clowns and witches,
Hunting for children,
Children hunting for candy,
And terrifying house luring you in.

Trick or treat?
Monsters hiding in every dark corner of the house,
They know you are there,
Waiting for the right moment to scare you,
Making you think your house is haunted,
They visit you in the woods,
They visit you in your dreams!

Trick or treat?
Boo! They are everywhere,
Spine-tingling screams that run through your head,
Who or what was it the night spirits come to play or
Is it the night of All Hallows' Eve?
Trick or treat?

Ellie-May Bourne (12) & Sophie Meese (13)
Grace Academy, Coventry

News Nuisance

Have you heard of killer clowns?
They are roaming around
Playing pointless pranks,
Nowhere near as dangerous as war's tanks

As pointless as killer clowns,
But what about those who drown in pain and suffering,
Danger and mayhem?

Hurricane Matthew destroying our lives,
Hurricane Matthew killing us like knives.
The rain is faster than bees fleeing from their hives.
Taking families, mothers and wives...

Why are we reporting on the nuisance news?
Killer clowns, pointless pranks and all things that may amuse.
While we listen to lie after lie our beautiful planet continues to die.
Pollution and disasters that take our lives,
Not reported and being left behind...

Austin Hudson (11)
Grace Academy, Coventry

The Girl In The Corner

Darkness loomed around me,
As the knife moved to me,
Why does no one care?
Why they don't even know I'm there?
Why should I even breathe the air?

As I walk down the endless corridors,
All I can see are the cracked floors,
Why does this remind me of my heart?
My broken, shrivelled heart,
Pumping as much blood as it can around my body.

A month has passed
I'm speaking out at last.
As I look down at my daughter's grave,
How can people be so cruel?
Why would they be fools?
Why do people bully human beings?
Don't they know that it hurts their feelings?
It is wrong and disgusting - it fills then up with pain
Would you like to be bullied?

Mya Devonish (12)
Grace Academy, Coventry

The Broken Girl

Be careful what you say,
A girl remembers everything,
A distant whisper in the crowd,
Can make a girl shut down.
Her designer clothing shouldn't mean a thing,
But what fits her is all she gets,
And that's all she brings.
She tries to change her image,
By altering herself,
But little did she know, this affected her health.
Bit by bit, she began to die,
Holding up all the secrets inside,
Of pain and agony she tried to hide.
It's as if all the love became the pain and the pain became the game,
That turned her fear into the hatred that was strong enough to break her,
They look at her like a stranger,
Yet worse,
The fragile soul she once saw,
Was hurt.

Sennya Paris Baalu (14)
Grace Academy, Coventry

Poetry Kills

Poverty bills, poverty kills,
All our money goes into tills,
My family trapped in a room like rats,
We have to sacrifice our lifestyle to live like bats.

My depressed parents cannot get a job
Which means we have to persistently rob,
Through the cold, harsh winters,
And the hot summer days,
My family do not still end up getting a pay.

My little brother is crying,
While my mum is uncomfortably lying
She is very slowly dying,
Surrounded by all the doctors and nurses sighing.

Her life is over now,
How could it happen? How?
We thought we could survive it together
But now it has taken her life forever,
Poverty bills, poverty kills...

Victoria Gurung (12) & Tamzin
Grace Academy, Coventry

Different

It's OK to be different

Everyone shouldn't be the same
If we were we would live in shame
Don't worry we're all not the same
Because if we were, we'd live in pain

People have problems
But it shouldn't stop their dreams
They shouldn't be treated any differently
Even though it all seems

People's differences don't leave mysteries
Everyone shouldn't believe the same
As we should all have different gains
Do you like being different?

Difference, difference, difference
It's all okay
Would you want to be the same?
It's all okay.

Amber-Rose Wogan (11)
Grace Academy, Coventry

Killer In The Basement

The blood
The gore
Guts suffocating the floor

The decapitated bodies
The gruesome pale heads
Sleeping on nail-made beds

Look up
Look down
Don't turn around

Hide upstairs
Hide left or right
Don't go downstairs into the basement

Pick up your flashlight
Turn it on brighter
Or you will be facing your long-awaited fate

Run up
Run outside
Don't stand staring or you'll be the predator's fresh meat bait

Off with your head
Straight off your shoulders
Blood all over the walls

The blood
The gore
Guts suffocating the floor.

Alfie Tolchard (12)
Grace Academy, Coventry

Coventry Football

Football,
A brilliant game with a ball,
You kick it,
You save it,
You smash it,
You score it,
It's a blast,
But the way City play,
Not Man City,
Coventry City,
Oh where do I kick off?
We have a horrid defence,
We have an awful midfield,
Our strike force,
They are as fast as a cheetah,
They are as strong as a rhino,
The fans make songs about them,
Like,
Sardel's on fire,
Your defence is terrified,
And our owner's Sisu,
Are having arguments,
Arguments about our stadium,
Sisu take my advice,

Pay out for some players,
Or pack up,
And leave!

Louis Ashby (12)
Grace Academy, Coventry

Make The World A Better Place

Fist-punch, foot crunch, hand hit, mouth spit, eyes swells, can't even see, please just let be me.
Through the doors and up the stairs, face all bloody, no one cares.
Everybody should be born equal and free with the ability to say I agree and disagree,
Everybody should have human rights - everyone, not just whites.
We need to reduce the amount of hunger and reduce the deaths of youngers.
We need stop the spread of malaria and get rid of dangerous bacteria.
We should make the environment nice and clean, and turn this world back to green.
If this was you what would you do? If you're not scared then spit your words too.

Ibrahima Diallo (13)
Grace Academy, Coventry

Robot Justice

I am a night guard, I am going to leave this place soon
There are robots trying to kill me
But there was the bite, the bite of 87
The purple guy killed seven children
And now they are looking for revenge
And now the robots are in the robot bodies
And now they are here for me, I am in a purple suit

Now it has been five nights I am safe
I have a new job, it's another robot place
I have to put my name into a key pad
There is something wrong with it
Now my name is Eggs Benedict
I have to zap some robots
It is night, five am, I am in a room called the Scooping Room
Now I am dead, the robots got their justice.

David Patrick (14)
Grace Academy, Coventry

Image

Click, click, pose, pose,
Is this how you want to live life?
Life behind the screen?
No reality.

Scrolling and controlling,
But the tears keep rolling.
People posing to drag you down,
People creating pictures that stream through your mind.

Do you realise what they are doing,
Showing off to a camera,
Winding up, winding down,
Acting like that model that was never one

Decorating their faces
Looking as fake as a Snapchat filter
Trying to create that false image

Don't let this be you,
Be yourself
And that is the person that people will love.

Bayleigh Reid (11)
Grace Academy, Coventry

Emotions Of The Week...

There are lots of days in the week,
Some are strong, some are weak.
It's your turn to decide,
Which one you would like to guide.

Monday is smiling as she's always happy,
Tuesday is crying as she's always sad.
Wednesday is moody as he's very snappy,
Thursday is evil, he's really bad!
Friday is tired as he's always sleepy,
Saturday is scared and it's kind of creepy.
Sunday is Sunday and she's always relaxing.

You choose which one you keep,
Or which one you lose,
Think about your family,
Think about your friends,
But hurry up!
Before your time ends.

Monica Chumber (11)
Grace Academy, Coventry

Depression

I hope nobody ever leaves
'Cause I don't want to be alone with me
I wish my anti-d lasted longer
I just need to be a little stronger
My mind is a dark place
It's as black as the vast space
In which we live we are living matter
But nothing we do will ever matter
In such a large universe we are but a speck
Sometimes I think about tying a noose around my neck
But I won't
But I can't
Why focus on the dark, why focus on the black
When there are people who will want me back?
Happiness is what we pursue
So I shouldn't feel blue
No need for a final letter because
It gets better.

Samuel Milligan (12)
Grace Academy, Coventry

Self-Image

Scrolling and scrolling,
Clicking and rolling,

Through pointless pics,
And pointless poses.
When will it stop?
When will it end?

Giving people false idols,
Just like a girl alone at home.
Feeling awful, feeling worthless,
Looking at Instagram on her phone.

School is like a nightmare
Where people are horrible.
Calling her as fat as a pig,
Saying she is dumb, pathetic, ugly.

Insults are bullets,
Your mouth a gun.
Words are valuable,
Don't waste them.
Be nice.
Be kind.
But most important, be yourself.
You don't need to change.

Kora Herbert (12)
Grace Academy, Coventry

Sports

Although the discrimination
Could have an effect on a nation
The players play
While the haters hate.
Messi might win
While Ronaldo goes top bins
They have to train
And go through the pain
So that they can retain the title
Steph curry hits a shot
And banks it in the pot
The crowd goes wild
While cheese goes mild
Coventry City is late on time
When Stormzy is making the latest grime
Liverpool hasn't won the league
Even though Leicester is in the Champions League
Lebron James making Ps
When Bournemouth is near the seas
Without a doubt
Cov wants Sisu out.

Zewelanji Sinkala (12)
Grace Academy, Coventry

Perseverance

I'm running, I'm sprinting,
I'm pushing ahead, I've got déjà vu
From that dream in bed.
My manager said that those hard
Courses would pay off, now here's
The finish line I just need to cross.

I'm hot on his heels,
I'm never gonna stop,
All I need is that last second
Steal to make him drop.
Like a rock.

Passion, none. Dedication,
None. When they say' I'm lazy
It's no pun.
I'm cold, I'm freezing, I'm out of the race,
The dirt off their heels
Is flying in my face.

Ravelle Berry (12)
Grace Academy, Coventry

Sports I Play

Serving, forehand, backhand, yet
Standing here ready for the set.
I play twice a week,
And now the strings are getting weak

Today I am playing cricket,
I hope I don't hit the wicket.,
We are playing the best team in the league
So now we are getting quite keen

In football my weakness is attacking,
However I am good at passing.
Each team needs defenders
So I guess I will be an attender

These are the sports I play
I try to play them every day
There is a lot of other sports to do
You should go and try them too.

Joshua James Townshend (12) & Tyler Griffiths (12)
Grace Academy, Coventry

Economic Worries

Economy, what has happened to it?
Corruption. Disorder. Fear. All over the fall of the pound,
The prices are rising on all pieces of ground,
Irrational idiots spread fear like a virus,
The answer is right in front of us,
All we need to do is...
Band together! Band together! Band together!

People keep worrying about going abroad,
You still can, just find a ship and hop aboard!
All of this is because of Brexit.
But there is no need to fear,
We will sort it out after about a year.
All we need to do is...
Band together! Band together! Band together!

Mitchell Tipple (11)
Grace Academy, Coventry

Stand Your Ground

I wear make-up to look beautiful like everyone else
You still don't like me, I put more and more and more on
But at the end of the day I'm just destroying myself and my confidence
So instead of putting myself down along with everyone else
I should stand my ground and say *no*
I'm not going to let everyone put me down.
Stand your ground.
Don't let people put you down because of your image
You are who you are
Love yourself
You only get one shot
Of life just keep your head up and smile
Live your life to the fullest and stand your ground.

Cheylene Edwards (14)
Grace Academy, Coventry

All About Make-Up

It's all about make-up!
Why can't we wake up?
And take up the fact,
That it's not all about make-up!
People say that you're ugly,

It's just jealousy!

Blusher, foundation, mascara,
Your face is like a concrete floor.
They say! 'You're fat like your mum'
They add to the insult.

They say, 'Every part of you is dumb!'
You see people you think are prettier
Than you on social media!
You're wishing you were the same.
It's just a plain make-up game!

Daisy Burke (11)
Grace Academy, Coventry

True Love

It all started that one day
When I got paid
He stared at me
I stared at him
He asked me if I want to meet him at three?
But where I asked?
He was nice and kind
He was hard to find
But I think I have found my true love
I can see the doves
Flying above
As happy as can be
We will love each other till we're sixty-three
As long as that can be
By each other's sides
Till the day we die
And forever lie
We grow up together
Have kids and many more
He's still my true love
And forever will be.

Sophie Baggott (12)
Grace Academy, Coventry

Self-Image

A world beyond the pixels on the screen,
A collage of beautiful people taking over social media.
People change to be someone else,
You change to be someone else.

Stop!
You are your own person who is unique and beautiful,
Why do you want to be someone else?
You make the world unique,
Don't make us all the same.

You have no confidence in yourself,
As you try to recreate the perfect selfie.
You realise you are not good enough,
Be confident in you because everyone else does.

Abi-Jo Healey (12)
Grace Academy, Coventry

Coventry

1000 fans cheering,
1000 fans fearing.
The players play and
The players hate.
Coventry still without any wins,
Sordell needs to hit one top bins.
Coventry lose again,
That's 10 out of 10.
Without a doubt
We want Sisu out!
Mowbray needs to pack
Because he's getting the sack.
Attackers can't score,
We need to show them the door.
Coventry have the youngest team,
But they never run out of steam.
Players have come and gone,
We just can't find the right one.

Thomas Ementon (12) & Spencer
Grace Academy, Coventry

Society

Does poverty really still exist?
Nameless people who won't be missed.
Every day someone dies,
Without getting to say goodbye.
Death, violence, guns and war,
Can society stand anymore?
Bang! Bang! Bang!
Gunshots echo throughout the land.
Anyone would do anything,
Under the Prime Minister's demand.
Society is falling apart,
Don't sit around, do something.

If we don't act now,
It could seal our fate.
Work together,
Before it's too late.

Alex Cooke (11)
Grace Academy, Coventry

Football

The brilliant game called football,
It brings us so much fun,
Especially when fast players are always on the run.
Liverpool, Man United and Leicester, they've all won
Don't you just hate it, when the 90 minutes is done?

For some it's just a game
For others it is passion
Some people play
Just for money for fashion

Although the game is great
And it is one that I rate
There is still room for hate
And hate is never in date.

Jack Nugent (13)
Grace Academy, Coventry

News

Breakfast, lunch and dinner is news, every day is news
If you don't have news
We won't know what happens today

Computers, tablets, phones and television has the news on
Telegraphs and magazines have news on
Trump: people call him mean, sexist, horrible and racist

The clowns are just playing pranks, the clowns are clowning around
The clowns have been called killers, murderous and nutters
When are the killer clowns going to stop?

Austin Kinmond (13)
Grace Academy, Coventry

Image

Fat, skinny, large or small,
On our silver screens we don't see that at all,
Tall, beautiful, make-up models,
Just what is their true potential?

Hiding themselves behind a curtain of make-up,
It just makes me want to shout to them, 'Wake up!'

Don't hide yourself under the covers,
Express who you are and people will discover,
It doesn't matter what you look like,
The whole point is to thrill and excite.

Emma Bagley (11)
Grace Academy, Coventry

Trump Vs Clinton

This poem is about Trump vs Clinton,
Trump wants to build a Mexico wall,
Hillary Clinton has pneumonia,
Why does the US have to vote for Donald Trump?
He is being racist and sexist,
I just think that Donald Trump is really, really disrespectful
Hillary Clinton wants to ban guns in the US,
Donald Trump and Hillary Clinton are going to a final
debate in Las Vegas,
Donald Trump's wife is sticking up for him.

Mya Phagura (14)
Grace Academy, Coventry

Every Day

Every day we wake up to a new day
Like we always see different things like rubbish
We never see the same car in the same place at the same time.
Running, skipping to school
Happy but sad, seeing everything around us in such a state.
It makes me think about people killing people
Hurt and suffering
Makes me wonder where the love is in the world.
Questioning myself what is going on.

Ryan Waring (13)
Grace Academy, Coventry

Homophobic Bullying

Homophobic
People say we are different,
Is it wrong being different?
Gay, bisexual, lesbian, straight,
We are all the same,
Doesn't matter who we are,
We are all different in our own ways.
Bullying
We are different,
Doesn't mean we should be bullied
Suicide,
People killing themselves
Is it fair?

Toni Pierce (13)
Grace Academy, Coventry

Childhood

At the age of three,
I was down on my knees,
Struggling with the pressure on the
Weight other than my shoulder,
Mother telling me I have to be bolder,
By 6 I was a terrible mix at school,
Bullied coming home not confessing,
Terrible nightmares consumed my brain day after day,
My papa said home is the place to go.

Alice McCarthy (12)
Grace Academy, Coventry

Trees Going Without Saying Bye

Trees going without saying bye,
But I just sat there trying to say hi,
Environment getting cut and chopped down,
I was too late to make my way down,

One by one,
My eyes have had enough,
All the animals are going to get down and hunt,
What will happen when my pencil goes blunt?

Bethanie Worrall (13)
Grace Academy, Coventry

Clowns

Be careful what you say,
The clowns are looking for prey,
Stab! Crack! Crunch!
The clowns are on the hunt,
Everywhere you go they are watching,
Everywhere you step they can hear you,
If you don't consider this now,
Your life will turn upside down.

Mackenzie Burnside (13)
Grace Academy, Coventry

Swearing

No swearing,
No cursing,
It makes me mad,
It's really bad.

It hurts me,
And it hurts others.
Even mothers
And daughters.

I want to cry,
Sometimes it's a lie.
It hurts my heart.
And it breaks apart!

Jordé Samuels (11)
Grace Academy, Coventry

Trump Versus Clinton

Him versus her.
Who will we choose?
The lesser of two evils
Will one ever lose?

Will we ever be able to escape the terrible fate
Of the two tyrants?
We might end up in a debate
In any event, will it all be too late?

Kristian Roberts (12)
Grace Academy, Coventry

Homework

Homework, homework, homework,
Where to begin,
That evil teacher says it's crucial
What a lie
'Waste of time'
She will deny.

We go home to rest
Not to learn
That's taking away our smile.

Kamrandeep Singh Lotta (12)
Grace Academy, Coventry

Do I Help The World?

I wake up in the morning
In my warm, cosy bed
But some people wake with only
The hard ground to rest their head.

I go downstairs
To my mother's warm embrace
But some people hide to get away
From their parents' face.

I sit down to drink clean water
And eat delicious food
But some people drink dirty water
And risk having an ill mood.

I go to school
To learn and grow
But some people can only wish to learn
The things I know.

I live in a home with great comfort
And good health
But some people live on the street
And have no wealth.

Some people only think of money
And greed
But others share their money
With people, who have mouths to feed.

Now take a look at yourself and say:
'Do I help the poor?
Do I help stop diseases from
Devastating more?

Do I help families
With mouths to feed?
Or do I sit around
And watch the world fall apart
By people
Consumed with greed?

Do I want to stop the wars
And bring peace and stop people
From being careless
Or do I watch and wait
For places to
Become nothing
But rubble and mess?

Katie Dodd (11)
Lyndon School, Solihull

This Needs To Stop

Sarah walks into school,
With no one but her teddy in her bag,
Everyone looking down at her,
Laughing at her,
Her head down,
Feeling nothing but afraid.

She sits on her own,
No one beside her,
People walking past,
Whilst she cries,
People staring,
Not asking if she's okay.

A young girl called Amy,
Sits next to her,
Amy is in Sarah's form,
They walk to form together,
Talking as if they are best friends,

They get to form,
Notes and balls of paper being thrown at Sarah,
'You're ugly,'
'Nobody likes you,'
She runs to the toilet,
With tears rushing down her face,
She can't stop,

This needs to stop,
Worrying to come to school,
Pretending to be sick,
Crying every day.

Amy rushes after her,
'Please don't cry,'
For once Sarah is out of the toilet,
Amy hugs her,
'Don't worry, I'm here,'
Sarah starts to have a smile on her face.
She is so grateful.

Kimberley Perks (13)
Lyndon School, Solihull

Help!

Help, that's all she wants
A solution to the problem she trapped herself in
Help, that's all she needs
To free herself from the monster within.

When a line is crossed and they've gone too far
How can this joke seem funny anymore?
A young girl with her whole life ahead
Or a nutcase with no chance of recovery.

Her parents say to fake a smile
It became easy for her after a while.
But the more she faked the more she cried
And tears fell every day and night.

With her last friend named hope fading away
She prepared for death and her final day
As her last moments arrived, she thought of:
How she tried
How she tried to love but failed every day.

Help, that's all she wanted
A solution to the problem she trapped herself in
Help that's all she needed
To free herself from the monster within!

Gemma Kane (13)
Lyndon School, Solihull

Animal Bullying

I see them being crushed
I see them in the grassy field
I see them being shot! *Pow!*
I see them in the foggy night.

I hear the trigger going back before they...

I hear them at night
I hear them screaming for help, they say goodbye
I hear them in the morning light
I hear them being crushed by the human eye

Let it go and all has gone!

I hope they survive
I hope I don't see their bad side
I hope they will not die
I hope I don't see them die side by side.

We see them every day
We see them in danger because of the men
We see them playing with their mom
We see them in our medicine.

Why kill our friends, can't we save them?
Can we save the little wolves
Because, we killed their mom?

Charlie White (11)
Lyndon School, Solihull

Listen

This is Jack
Jack going to stab you in the back
Jack thinks you're a sssssnake
Jack thinks you're fake
Your life is really low
I have more importance in my toe
You need to pull yourself together
Because nothing is forever.

So what if I'm white
Does that make it wrong or right?
So what if I'm tall, so what if he's small
What's that got to do with life?
Maybe he's Muslim, maybe he's Sikh
Maybe he doesn't know the days of the week
So what if he's stupid, so what if he's smart?
Does that mean you can separate them apart?

Imagine a life with no heart
Imagine a life, split apart
Don't be racist, rude or fake
Be kind to others, give and take
You'll find your personality deep down in your soul
So if you feel lonely dig out of that hole.

Lucy Thomas (14) & Charly Curran (13)
Lyndon School, Solihull

The Way I Am

Everybody sees me from the outside
There's more to me than anybody knows
Misunderstood and judged,
The increasing feeling of being alone.

I'm not one of you
There's a different path I have to take
But what you have to understand is,
It's not my fault I'm the way I am.

So don't hate me for what I am,
Accept me for what I want to be,
I'm not going to change from what you can see,
The only person I can be is me.

I walk on my own, talking to no one
Avoiding the look in your eyes.
I'm not going to change for anyone.
I will hold onto my pride
Holding my head up high.

So don't hate me for what I am
Accept me for what I want to be
I'm not going to change for what you can see
The only person I can be is me.

Aaliyah Kay (12)
Lyndon School, Solihull

Stop And Think

He's standing there,
With a smile on his face,
Is it real?
Or is it fake?

You can clearly tell
By the tears in his eyes,
Tears of joy,
You can tell he's about to cry!

Cry for his family,
Cry for his friends,
For them in the war,
It could be the end!

As the pennies fall into his bucket,
Each sound reminds him,
About devastation in his family,
In the war, they are suffering!

But the tears in his eyes,
Say more than just that,
There's a whole story behind them,
And it is nothing but fact!

He has experienced a lot,
Wars, bombs and missiles,
So give him some hope,
It is surely worth your while!

Please stop and think,
Even for a moment,
Please stop and think,
Before everything goes silent...

Amnah Hussain (12)
Lyndon School, Solihull

Loved Forever

As I cry, you soothe me
As I roll, you support me
As I crawl you guide me
As I toddle, you reward me
As I talk, you teach me.

As I run, you watch me
As I ride, you stabilise me
As I error, you scold me
As I succeed, you cheer me
As I leave, you weep.

But the story continues on,
Far as long as love itself
A journey of love and trust,
Hand in hand, never by myself,
Through thick and thin, always by my side.

When I cry, you soothe me
When I return, you support me
When I struggle, you guide me
When I attain, you reward me
When I error, you teach me.

When I marry, you watch me
When I worry, you stabilise me
When I misjudge, you scold me
When I succeed, you cheer me
When you go, I weep.

Nikitha Kaur Jheeta (12)
Lyndon School, Solihull

A Girl's Disguise

She wakes up in the morning,
And puts on her mask,
Red lips, blue eyes and blonde curled hair,
She fixes her tie then goes downstairs,
She heads for the kitchen,
For something to eat,
Says hi to her mum,
But her mum doesn't listen,
So she walks out the door,
And heads for school,
She says hi to her friends,
And her friends - they all listen,
She smiles and laughs and pretends it's okay,
But they don't know the pain she's taken,
They don't see the smile she's faking,
So she heads to school,
And it's fine for a while,
Then she goes home,
And opens the door,
Takes a punch to the stomach,
And throws up her food from school,
At school where she's fine,
And her friends - they all listen.

Simran Ajimal (13)
Lyndon School, Solihull

Differences!

Fruit, they're all different,
Apples, pears, strawberries, mangoes, oranges,
They are all different colours, tastes, shapes, sizes,
That's exactly the same with us.

We are all different,
Shape, size, weight, height,
But we all have something,
We have the ability to be great,
We have the ability to believe,
And we have the ability to be capable of anything
But only, if we try.

So the next time you laugh
At someone, just stop and think
They can be capable of lots of great things
They could be a famous rock star in a Hollywood dream,
And who would be laughing then, you? Them?

So don't be a hater or a doubter,
Be a listener,
Be a believer...

Jessica Rogers (11)
Lyndon School, Solihull

War

So many wars, all around the world,
On the news every day,
War
War
War
Syria, Iraq, families broken,
A token to a better world
If only
Children left lonely,
To care for themselves,
Parents killed, trying to run
Shot down dead in front of their children
They are now orphaned
No one to care for them
Don't have privileges
Quite like we do,
No food to eat,
No toys to play with,
I dream of a world without war
A world of peace
A world where everyone has a place to live,
I have my family, some people don't,
They should have lives too,
But sadly, they don't.

Marcus Walker (13)
Lyndon School, Solihull

The Happiness A Pet Can Bring

I see him in the morning,
His little furry face,
The sound of his purr as I tie my lace,
Then I say goodbye and set off for school.
I long to go home and pray I see you soon,
There you are in my doorstep after school,
You eat dinner with me,
Watch TV with me,
Until it's time for bed,
Sweet dreams my kitty.
Were the last words I said.
I woke up yet again a normal holiday,
I looked around and you were not here to play,
My dear sweet kitty
Who was a friend and family too
I didn't know what to do
'Mother, Mother!' I screamed
Last time I saw my dear kitty, he was buried in mud and leaves.

Hira Ahmed (13)
Lyndon School, Solihull

Corrupting Peace

We are all different
That's what makes us the same
But people don't get this
That's what makes them insane!
Terrorists, extremists - are all inhumane
Causing the innocent to be in pain
They do this for fun
Not for money or gain
They live their life happily
But they should be ashamed...

On the news, we see them there
Holding hostages but they don't care
Everywhere we go there's a danger
From suicide bombers to a kidnapping stranger
Terrorist attacks are coming more and more
The toleration has ended
Now it's a war.

Yusuf J Choudhury (12)
Lyndon School, Solihull

World Education

At 1 I learnt to say Mommy and Daddy
At 2 I learnt to walk
At 3 I learnt to say 1 to 10
At 4 I learnt to speak
At 5 I learnt to say the alphabet
At 6 I learnt to write my name
At 7 I learnt to add 9 and 8
At 8 I leant to tell the time
At 9 I learnt punctuation
At 10 I learnt to write poetry
At 11 I learnt to debate
At 12 I learnt Pythagorean
At 13 I leant how to pass an exam

School's hard.
Learning to read, write, do maths,
History, French verbs, world geography
And how to form my own opinion.

But I'm lucky.

Sinead Murphy (13)
Lyndon School, Solihull

Magazine Girls

I read the magazines
See models on every page
How perfect they all look
A fake smile on each one's face.

The perfect skin tone?
It doesn't exist
But the girls on the pages say:
'It looks like this.'

They say everyone is beautiful,
If you look a certain way.

None of it is real though...
The way they look.

Faces coated in make-up
Hair tied up so tight they're in pain!
Forced fake smiles
And pricey designer clothes.

All to have it photoshopped,
And made to look even worse.

Harriet Tatem (12)
Lyndon School, Solihull

The War Life

Boom!
There was another bomb,
Scrambling, scampering, scurrying away.

Click! Click! Bang!
There's another death
As the soldiers drop, grasping for their last breath...

One soldier just joined
One baby just crawled

One soldier just dropped
One baby just jumped

Some people grow,
Others die...

31 soldiers joined
30 soldiers died

One left alive
Shot down, struck down

Stranded, all alone
Hand on heart, staring into the sky as he takes his last breath...

Aryaan Ahmed (12)
Lyndon School, Solihull

War

Why?
Why war?
It just makes us hate,
More and more.

Tank, shells and bombs,
Rifle rounds and weeping moms.
Bullets whizz over innocent heads,
Tanks roll up on the field,
People dying in their beds.

Look to your left,
Someone's loading a mortar.
Look to your right,
Civilians crying for water.

People back home saying, they've got a hard time,
With bills and tax.
But never been hit,
By a roadside mine.

Why?
Why war?
It just makes us hate,
More and more.

Eliot Gambino (12)
Lyndon School, Solihull

Real Beauty

Why do we feel the need to be plastic, emotionless?
Anxiety flooding our brains, hopes, dreams.

Scarring our faces with surgery, make-up, fear,
Only to feel equal, confident.

God made us who we are for a reason
We should feel the strength to hold our head up high.

We are unique from our head to our toes
From our hearts to our souls.

Our passion, our fear, what we love to hate
To cry or smile

We are all beautiful inside

We may not see our beauty,
But when we do we're unstoppable.

Sophie Monnington (12)
Lyndon School, Solihull

Changes

The world is so beautiful,
So delicate,
Like glass,
A picture of perfect colours,
Blending into each other,
Forests of green,
Fields of yellow,
Nature coats the floor like a blanket...
Landscapes collide,
Love bonds...

Yet sides of people can change,
Helpless animals become trophies
Nature becomes a blur,
Selfish minds,
Fire burns,
Disease spreads,
Poverty kills
Heaven becomes Hell,
Breathtaking views become horrifying

People can be cruel,
Dreams are becoming nightmares...

Lily Faye Shemmans (11)
Lyndon School, Solihull

Does It Matter?

Does it matter if you're mixed race?
No
Does it matter if you're small?
No
Does it matter if you wear glasses?
No
Does it matter if you have big ears?
No
Does it matter if you have squinty eyes?
No
Does it matter if you have ginger hair?
No.

You are you.
Don't ever change
It's okay to be different
No need to rearrange
Don't alter yourself because of the bullies
They only do it because they are dummies.
You are special in every way
So you should be you every day.

Summer McDonald (11)
Lyndon School, Solihull

I Was Depressed

I stabbed him
I had enough,
I was depressed,
What other way can it be?
Life or death,
He lay there,
Cold as ice,
He's gone,
Gone for good,
I ask myself why,
Time and time,
Over and over again,
I already said,
I was depressed,
Overthinking,
It's killed my happiness,
Killed my freedom,
I feel the tight grip,
The stone-cold cuffs,
Getting tighter and tighter,
It locked, you heard the click,
I held my head in shame,
I was depressed.

Matty Richardson
Lyndon School, Solihull

Face

She rolls from her bed,
Hair a mess and skin that's red
She looks into the glass that shows her true reflection,
Dull, brown eyes and blotchy complexion.
A cylinder of pale liquid
Tipped onto a brush
Porcelain powder piled on in a rush.
Her rounded cheeks become sharp and drawn.
The eyebrows painted on, no longer a ghost.
Black wings on her eyes and the pink shadows on her lid
Are what compliments her orbs the most.
With one last glance in the glass
She's happy with her mask.

Maisy Smith (13)
Lyndon School, Solihull

Bully Boys

I see a group of boys,
They push me down,
They whack me, hit me,
Kick me to the ground.

I walk around the playground,
They stare at me,
They pull me, push me,
Send me to my knees

I come out of school,
They take my phone off me,
They throw me to the ground,
They stamp all over me.

As I walked into my house,
My mom said to me,
'It's going to be okay,
I'm here if you need me.'

Elle Burrows (11)
Lyndon School, Solihull

Social Media

Social media:
Is the way to go
To find out knowledge
Of the world we know.

On Facebook, Snapchat and Instagram
Some will bare all
People who you think you know
You really don't know them at all.

Internet safety
Must always be used
Otherwise you're opening yourself up
To be trolled and abused.

Social media
Is a joyous interaction
But used in the wrong way
Brings dissatisfaction.

Millie Victoria Hoare (12)
Lyndon School, Solihull

Animal Cruelty

The animals' skin black and blue;
With their ribs sticking out.
Sad eyes looking through the cage,
Begging for food and water just to survive;
Whimpering quietly under their breath.

Imagine how would you like to be
Locked in a cage not being able to run free,
Like the animals you can hear from outside,
Your stomach rumbling, on the edge of dehydration.
Think if you would like to be abused
Before you hurt another living thing.

Jessica-Mai Bird (12)
Lyndon School, Solihull

Hey Dad

Hey Dad
Hey son
Happy birthday son
Thanks Dad

Later that day
Hey son
Hey Mom
It weren't Dad
Where is he?
Mom
Said
Son, Dad died
Sinking, feeling inside
Last thing he said
See you later, love you.
But later didn't come.

Hey Dad
Hey son
Happy birthday son
Thank's Dad

Bye Dad
Bye son
Until we meet again
Love you Dad.

Luke Bancroft (14)
Lyndon School, Solihull

Why Is It OK To Be Different?

Glasses, no glasses, we all cry,
Long fingers, short fingers, we all write.
Fat, skinny, we all eat.

In our world we all have different qualities,
Techniques and talents.
Who cares if you're not good at maths?
We all learn in different ways.

No hair, long hair, we are all pretty wonderful in our own way.
Whether it's to whistle or sing, on top of a building.
We all have different ways to spend our time.

Kiera Reeves (12)
Lyndon School, Solihull

I'm Only A Little Different...

I know I look a little scary,
But there's no need to be wary,
I know I'm different,
That doesn't mean you can stare,
I will defend myself with my breathtaking glare,
But that doesn't mean I don't care,
I really want a friend,
Again and again people run and laugh,
Secretly I'm just like you,
Think about it you have bones inside you,
I just have the outside,
I'm only a little different.

Leah May Howes (11)
Lyndon School, Solihull

Start Again

They beat me up
Punch me in the face,
Ask me for money
Make fun of my race.

They make fun of my mum and dad,
They treat me so bad.
Please put me somewhere,
Where I will be glad.

I struggle here, falling to pieces
Begging on my knees,
For someone to help me
Will you please?

I can't stay,
I am such a big disgrace
I need to run away
I need to start again.

Hashim Rashid (13)
Lyndon School, Solihull

By Himself

He sits there by himself,
Scared, lonely
Pushed out of the back queue
Bullied, beaten up,
Don't know what to do.

He sits there by himself
Quiet, lonely
Bullied every day,
Punched in the face,
They call him names, ugly, dumb and gay.

He sits there by himself,
Quiet, lonely,
They say he's got no friends
They say he's a low life,
No life.

Gurkirpal Bansal (13)
Lyndon School, Solihull

It's OK To Be Different

Me, Grim Reaper
I'm from the Underworld.
People are so scared of me,
I make their arm-hair curled.
When I sat down people gave me the looks,
However, I'm not not part of that gang of crooks.
Looking around, they see my face is white,
Everyone avoiding me to get rid of the fright.
Black cape,
Crooked teeth,
Smelly breath too,
But believe me I'm normal,
Just like you.

Yousuf Awwal (11)
Lyndon School, Solihull

My Reflection Is A Monster!

I stand in front of the mirror
And only see a monster instead of me.

My head's too big
My lips are too small
My stomach is popped out
My legs are bulky
My hair is too curly.

Why would anyone want to be my friend.
Why can't I be like the girls in the magazines?
Is there a way I can be photoshopped?
Why do I have to be me?

I hate me!

Maham Hassan (13)
Lyndon School, Solihull

Suffragettes

They fought for their rights
Though people shunned the fights
They fought to be equal
But people wanted a sequel
Of fights, that shouldn't be fought
And laws, that couldn't be bought.

They knew they would succeed,
Because they planted the seed
In the mind of the people
Who did not want to be equal.
How hard would it be
To share the responsibility
With me?

Maisie Haddock-Garey (13)
Lyndon School, Solihull

Animal Cruelty

Bang!
The helpless dog is whimpering on the floor,
While the cruel owner stands snickering out the door.
Body bleeding.
The poor dog's screeching.
He's done nothing wrong to get a beating,
Is this what you want our world to be?
A brutal world where animals flee.
No I don't think so.
Why do we do it?
Together we can put an end to...

Animal cruelty!

Tatum Alicia Smith (12)
Lyndon School, Solihull

Fantastic Father

Anchors beneath the ocean are very strong,
That's what you are to me, Father.

Tanks slowly making their way to war very strongly,
That's what you are to me, Father.

Superheroes flying in the sky going to save the day,
That's what you are to me, Father.

The favourite part of my day is coming home and seeing my father,
Because you're my hero.

Lewis Watkins (11)
Lyndon School, Solihull

Different

I hate the way you stare
That disgusted glare
Sometimes I feel it's not quite fair

You shove me into the corner
A prisoner to your word
Sometimes I feel like it can't get worse

When being yourself causes you pain
You've got to get up again
Because no matter what they say
Just remember, being yourself is okay.

Ella Hutchins (11)
Lyndon School, Solihull

Bullying

Don't let your tears fall,
Don't let your spirit break,
Doesn't matter what they say,
Just stay strong, just stay strong, just stay strong

Don't keep it in,
Don't shy away,
Don't let the bullies get their way,
The bullies are the ones to blame.

Isobel Douglas (11)
Lyndon School, Solihull

What Is This?

Wars are depressing,
Wars are cruel,
Why do people need to take over,
Why do people need to rule,
Soldiers fight for us,
Soldiers die for us,
All because of an unwanted guest,
Moms crying,
Citizens dying,
Why do we need war?
It's just anger.

Amy Stretton (12)
Lyndon School, Solihull

The Quiet Girl

5 years old,
As happy as can be,
Every day was her own,
Back then she didn't see,
The bad world she lived in.

Her hair in plaits,
A constant smile,
She knew nothing different than that -
What was a frown?

10 years old,
A forced laugh,
Every day she tried harder,
Parents always spoke on her behalf,
Crowded by people, but alone
She began to understand the comfort of cold air,
What was wrong and right?

15 years old,
Stress brought her headaches,
Every day just dragged,
Believed that every person was a snake.
Everything changed.

Boys broke her heart,
Girls made her shake,

The only thing she wondered was...
Will I ever get a break?

20 years old,
It's a different story,
The glint came back to her eyes,
Love by her side and
A warmth in her heart.

She prayed for herself,
Nobody else,
'You never know pain until you've passed it,
You never know happiness until you have it.'
She said, what was a smile?

Melek Morris (13)
Lyng Hall School, Coventry

Untitled

When I was 12, I knew I was still confused
With life,
How everyone knew what they wanted
To be,
Teacher, police officer, architect.
There was something about these jobs which
Wasn't really me.

Then I took a long to think about what
I want,
I realised then, I didn't want to face it alone.
My eyes were captivated by the ray of sunshine, shining on my family.
They were the battery to my phone!

They thought I could be a lawyer,
Fighting through my life to the finish line,
Believing myself to complete the obstacle courses of life
Knowing I could lead this job until I'm 99.

Anesah Akhtar (12)
Lyng Hall School, Coventry

My Views On Society

Society is cruel, spiteful and evil
Almost as cruel as the times called medieval

People tend to use hurtful labels
Those can make people feel worse than horses in stables

Why can't others have their own view on the world?
Maybe some are religious or believe in the Underworld

Perhaps you should be less judgemental of other people
'Cause at this point, your 'jokes' are nothing but feeble

Your words can break hearts
Or tear their souls apart

They tend to cry in solitude
Their friends barely keep them glued
You're like the Joker, laughing at others' pain
Why don't you make a pencil disappear into someone's brain

All 'labels' should be praised
At least they have confidence, that's how we should be raised.

Because of this world, people develop anxiety
This is a huge understatement on my views of society.

Mia Smith (12)
Willenhall E-ACT Academy, Willenhall

War Is Strong Enough To Break

War is strong enough
To break a
Heart to
Break a
Moral to
Ruin a life
To ruin a soul,
As the shells whizz past as fast as light,
I feel myself breaking, giving into this fight.
The ground shakes beneath me, scaring my wit,
The massacre of people blown to bits
War is strong enough
To break a
Heart to
Break a
Moral to
Ruin a life
To ruin a soul
A juxtaposition, this is what it is, like a castle crumbing,
The words just don't fit,
My feelings and emotions slowly drifting away
However adrenaline running through me helps me live another day.
War is strong enough
To break
A heart

To break
A moral
To ruin a life
To ruin a soul,
Screaming and gunshots, the only sound to be heard
Humans are ruthless, careless, helpless however absurd.
War is strong enough
To break
A heart
To break
A moral
To ruin a life
To ruin a soul,
Senses are fading, blue fingers are numb
My sanity is leaving, I'm just listening to the sound of the gun.
War is strong enough to break,
And I know that it's true,
You will never understand until it's you,
War is strong enough to break a heart,
Yes when my family discover me scarred,
Scarred and broken from the painful and hard...
War is strong enough to break...

Abigail Carnegie (12)
Willenhall E-ACT Academy, Willenhall

Animal Abuse

Humans are throwing their spears,
Everywhere us hyenas go.
The animals are shedding tears,
They are laughing as they kill us off,
One
By
One.

It's torture to us animals.
Save the herd!
Save us all!

We are surviving,
As we yelp for help,
We go helping the fallen.
They are picking the pups off,
The bullets tunnelling through our hearts.

No one's safe,
As we run,
The rocks hurt our paws,
Along with the dead corpses.
The blood of our families,
Is all around the savannah.

The bulls are crowding the humans,
Some are protecting us.
The humans jump in their cars,
They got what they came for.
We weep in despair.

Sophie Roberts-Maybury (12)
Willenhall E-ACT Academy, Willenhall

Bullying

I stood on the deserted playground,
I had no money on me,
I saw the monster coming close,
There's nowhere to flee.

I'm dreading school like a nightmare,
Not wanting to leave the house,
Eventually I have to.
I travel to school with sweat on my blouse.

I'm fed up with this,
It's not fair on me.
The wind howled in anger.
I should be accepted for being me!

I am stronger,
I don't care if you don't agree.
I am the best version of me that I can possibly be!

Jade Olivia Wall (12)
Willenhall E-ACT Academy, Willenhall

Identity

Identity, identity. Can I find my identity?

Tall, short, thin, big?
Am I unique or am I the same?
No matter if we are the same, our DNA is different.

Loud, quiet, angry, happy.
Our feelings will always be different.

Our qualities and our beliefs and our expressions make us different.
They enable us to find our identity.

Identity, identity.
I'm starting to grasp my identity.

Kelis Cutrera (11)
Willenhall E-ACT Academy, Willenhall

YOUNG WRITERS INFORMATION

We hope you have enjoyed reading this book – and that you will continue to in the coming years.

If you're a young adult who enjoys reading and creative writing, or the parent of an enthusiastic poet or story writer, do visit our website **www.youngwriters.co.uk.** Here you will find free competitions, workshops and games, as well as recommended reads, a poetry glossary and our blog.

If you would like to order further copies of this book, or any of our other titles, then please give us a call or visit **www.youngwriters.co.uk.**

Young Writers
Remus House
Coltsfoot Drive
Peterborough
PE2 9BF
(01733) 890066
info@youngwriters.co.uk